Truly & Cheesy™
Romans in Britain
Facts & Jokes

It's a cut above!

*It's a l

Published in Great Britain in MMXVIII by
Book House, an imprint of
The Salariya Book Company Ltd
25 Marlborough Place, Brighton BN1 1UB
www.salariya.com

ISBN: 978-1-912233-02-1

SALARIYA

1 3 5 7 9 8 6 4 2

A CIP catalogue record for this book is available
from the British Library.

Printed and bound in China.
Printed on paper from sustainable sources.

Created and designed by
David Salariya.

Visit
www.salariya.com
for our online catalogue and
free fun stuff.

PAPER FROM
SUSTAINABLE
FORESTS

Author:
John Townsend worked as a
secondary school teacher before
becoming a full-time writer.
He specialises in illuminating and
humorous information books for
all ages.

Artist:
David Antram studied at
Eastbourne College of Art and then
worked in advertising for 15 years
before becoming a full-time artist.
He has illustrated many children's
non-fiction books.

Truly Foul & Cheesy™ Romans in Britain

Facts & Jokes

This Truly Foul & Cheesy
book belongs to:

....

Written by

John Townsend

Illustrated by

David Antram

BOOK HOUSE
a SALARIYA imprint

Introduction

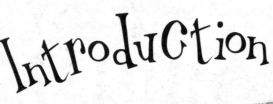

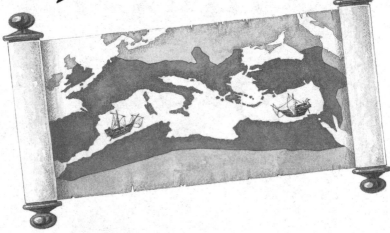

Warning – reading this book might not make you **LOL** (laugh out loud) but it could make you **GOL** (groan out loud), feel sick out loud or **SEL** (scream even louder). If you are reading this in a library by a **SILENCE** sign… get ready to be thrown out!

Disclaimer: The author really hasn't made anything up in this book (apart from some daft limericks and jokes). He checked out the foul facts as best he could and even double-checked the fouler bits to make sure – so please don't get too upset if you find out something different or meet any Romans, ancient Britons or historians gabbling in Latin who happen to know better. And if a gladiator tells you anything at all… RUN!

If I had my way, I'd RATify the lot!'

Official Warning

This book contains a bizarre mixture of wacky facts (some foul and cringy), as well as corny comments, jokes and puns about when the Romans invaded and ruled much of Britain for almost 400 years. Before many thousands of Roman soldiers arrived in 43 AD, they called native Britons a rowdy rabble who 'dye themselves with woad*, which occasions a bluish colour, and thereby have a more terrible appearance in fight. They wear their hair long, and have every part of their body shaved except their head and upper lip.' So said Julius Caesar himself (the Roman dictator who first tried to invade Britain in 55 BC).

*woad = a plant of the cabbage family, grown in ancient Britain for making blue dye.
The Romans referred to Ancient Britons as 'Picts', which is Celtic for painted or tattooed.

From Rome, Britain was far across the sea, but with her own tempting gold and tin. Maybe the emperor's wife said, 'I want her riches. Julius – seize her!' (Yes, that's how bad the puns are in this book.) So, get ready for plenty of daft, scary, foul and revoltingly cheesy facts with jokes. Be prepared to visit Britain when things were often gross or worse.

Limerick Time

With the Romans, how we've all
become smitten,
As so many books have been written
But none quite like this
(Be prepared for sheer bliss)
As you read about
'Romans in Britain'
(with extra foul and cheesy
bits included)

In the Beginning...

Before the Romans arrived, Britain was inhabited by scattered tribes of Celts. The word Celt comes from the Greek word, Keltoi, which means barbarians, and is pronounced as 'Kelt'. They weren't called Celts at the time – the Romans called them Britons (or something much ruder) and described them like this:

'They are very tall in stature, with rippling muscles under clear white skin. Their hair is blond, but not naturally so: they bleach it, to this day, artificially, washing it in lime and combing it back from their foreheads. They look like wood-demons, their hair thick and shaggy like a horse's mane. Some of them are clean-shaven, but others – especially those of high rank – shave their cheeks but leave a moustache that covers the whole mouth.'
Diodorus Siculus (A Roman historian)

Maybe your ancestors were as scary as this!

Riddle Time

Why does it always rain in Britain?

Q: When the Roman Emperor asked what weather to expect in Britain, what did they say?

A: 'Hail, Caesar.' (Or maybe 'There'll be an awful lot of reigning!')

Q: When the Romans first arrived in Britain, how do we know they often got lost?

A: Because the Britons found them Roman (roamin') all over the place.

Q: What did the ancient Britons say when the Romans arrived?

A: Don't lat-in that lot! (Actually, ancient Britons didn't speak English – but yes, the Romans spoke and wrote in Latin.)

Daft Joke

When the Romans began attacking the Celts in Wales, they were set upon by a single brave Welsh warrior with a club in one hand and a rock in the other. Eventually, with hundreds of soldiers launching an attack, they managed to force him to retreat into a cave. They followed him inside… but immediately everyone ran out again, bleeding and screaming: 'It's a trap! There's two of them!' After all, no one messes with a couple of Celts!

(The Welsh have the Romans to thank for bringing leeks to Britain – the leek is now the emblem of Wales)

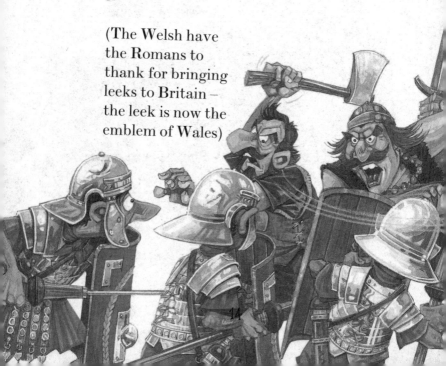

Daft Limerick

When the Romans arrived
from warm Italy,
They complained of the cold
very bitterly,
Turning blue as they strode...
'It's the end of the woad!'
Laughed the blue-painted
Britons, so wittily.

Ready for some foul
stuff now? What else
did you expect in a
book of foul facts?
Here goes:

1 The inhabitants of ancient Rome
had a sewer goddess, a toilet god
and a god of excrement.

2 The Romans used powdered mouse brains
as toothpaste – or even urine to whiten
their teeth (just right for a wee smile).
They also sloshed plenty of the warm liquid
into their tubs when washing clothes. The
ammonia in urine helped with cleaning,
and pots were left outside shops and public
urinals to collect public pee donations.

3 The public toilets in Rome were often disgusting. They were probably never cleaned and full of parasites. Romans using the toilets would have to take in special combs for scraping out lice from their skin and hair. The toilets were shared with lots of people, all sitting together, with just one sponge on a stick for passing round to wipe each bottom, without being washed in between. Nice.

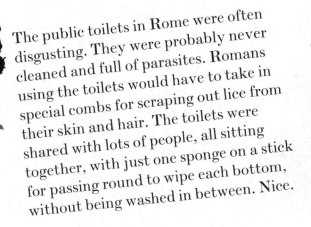

Ergh - I've got hold of the wrong end of the stick.

4 Life expectancy in Ancient Rome for many people was only about 20 to 30 years (not surprising if they spent much time in the public toilets).

17

The Roman Empire

Quick reminders

- The great Roman Empire all started in Italy's city of Rome in 753 BC and lasted for well over 1,000 years. During that time, Rome grew to rule much of Europe, Western Asia and Northern Africa. The Romans had a lasting impact on all of these places, where there are still many remains of Roman objects and buildings.

- The Roman Empire finally fell in 476 AD when the last Roman Emperor (Romulus Augustus) was defeated by the German Goth Odoacer – and 'the Dark Ages in Europe' began.

- Roman girls often got married at the age of 14. A father chose his daughter's husband for her and she wouldn't be allowed to disagree.

- Some rich Romans loved to feast on such delights as jellyfish, boiled ostrich, stuffed sow's udder and flamingo boiled with dates. Apparently, one popular dish was larks' tongues – the recipe required 1,000 of the birds. Sometimes a slave would bring round a sick bowl between courses. After all, they had to make room for pudding.

Who'd like more flamingo trifle?

Roman Medicine

Could be both foul and daft — with 'cures' like:

 Slap a cobweb on a wound to stop the bleeding.

OUCHH!

 Rub tar and animal urine on the head to cure baldness.

3 Slap a nice piece of liver on the eyes if they get sore.

4 Kiss a mule's nostrils to stop hiccups (your hiccups, not the mule's).

5 If in doubt, chew a lump of garlic and dribble all that garlic-spit on any sore areas.

Gross Limerick

If Romans ate more than their fill,
Clogged up their insides and felt ill,
They had lots of potions
To loosen their motions...
Or, if push came to shove, a huge drill!

(True – Romans used drills to remove diseased bits of bone, to drill through the skull for basic brain surgery and to remove weapons stuck in bones. It's best not to try this yourself!)

Silly Riddles

Q: What do you call a Roman with a cold?
A: Julius Sneezer.

Q: Where did Julius Caesar keep his armies?
A: Up his sleevies.

Q: How did the ancient Romans cut their hair?
A: With a pair of Caesars.

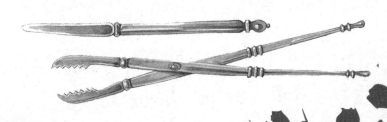

Romans on the Move

The Roman Army was always being sent off to conquer new lands. Soldiers were well-paid but it was a tough life – especially when they marched to hostile places far from home – like Britain. In fact, it took three attempts for the Romans to conquer Britain. Julius Caesar tried to invade twice, in 55 BC and the following year. His ships were wrecked in storms and when they eventually landed on the Kent coast, they had to fight the local 'barbarians'.

It took nearly 100 years before the Romans dared to return.

In 43 AD, Emperor Claudius sent 40,000 soldiers across the English Channel, even though many of them were terrified. The full might of the Roman army landed on the beaches in Kent and began battling inland, chopping down anyone who stood in their way. The Romans wanted Britain's precious metals. They called the land 'Britannia', which meant 'land of tin'. As they spread through the country, they built forts, new towns and roads. They also spread their culture, laws, language – and public toilets.

Watch Your Language

The Romans spoke Latin so their words began to shape the language spoken all around Britain. Today, much of the English language is rooted in Latin, because the Normans invaded in 1066, speaking French, which is also based on Latin. So, be prepared to try some Latin right now. If the Romans brought this book to Britain with them, they wouldn't call it 'Truly Foul Facts and Cheesy Jokes' but 'Vere Foedis Factis et Iocos Caseus'. (In fact, that really means 'cheese jokes' so it's maybe best to say 'iocos miserabilis'. You can probably work out what that means.)

Get ready for a FIGHT

When the Romans invaded, they met Celtic tribes that tried to fight back. In 60 AD, a native leader raised a huge army. She was Queen Boudicca of the Iceni tribe. Her forces went on a rampage, burning the Roman towns of Colchester and London, before heading north to St Albans. When the Roman army heard about this, they turned back from their campaign in Wales to face Boudicca. Even though the Romans were outnumbered by Boudicca's 200,000 warriors, they were better trained and had better armour. Both sides clashed in a fierce battle, but the Romans eventually won. Romans 1, Britons 0. Boudicca dead. She either killed herself to avoid capture, or died of illness (maybe she used too many Roman toilets).

ARRGGHHH!

29

Can You Believe It?

About 70,000–80,000 Romans and British were killed in the battles led by Boudicca. All this trouble made Emperor Nero think about withdrawing all Roman forces from Britain. But once Boudicca was out of the way, the Romans carried on invading more areas.

Most Britons in southern Britain settled down to Roman order and discipline. Towns grew up across the country, including York, Chester, St. Albans, Bath, Lincoln, Gloucester and Colchester. All of these major centres are still linked today by roads built by the Romans, all radiating from the port of London. The Romans were now here to stay.

By the way

- A foul fact about Nero (Emperor from 54 to 68 AD).

A few Roman emperors were totally bonkers. Nero was one of them. He didn't like his mother much so he tried to poison her – three times. Each time he failed so it was Plan B. He made the ceiling collapse on her. She survived. Plan C was to sink the ship she was on. She survived. In the end, he sent his soldiers to stab her to death. What a nice man. When Nero tried to kill himself, he failed again. His servant had to finish him off instead. What a loser.

TEST-

to see if you're paying
attention...

Q: Nero was the fifth
Emperor of Rome. Who
was the one before him?

A: The fourth! Actually, Nero
followed Claudius (who led
the invasion of Britain).

Map of

Britain

showing key Roman sites

Hadrian's wall

Ebroracum

Caistor

Letocetum

Viroconium   Wall

Glevum   Durovernum

Moridunum

Noviomagus

Isca

Dumovana

Did You Know?

The Romans never got around to conquering Ireland, probably because they were just too busy sorting out all the scary tribes in England, Wales and Scotland. They must have looked across the sea to Ireland and thought they'd invade one day. But in the first century AD, they already had enough on their hands.

Wales

If there's one thing the Romans couldn't stand, it was a Druid. A Druid was a priest or magician in the ancient Celtic religion. There were quite a few Druids in Wales, so the Romans went after them. A grisly attack on the island of Anglesey in 60 AD wiped out most of the Druids there. It was one of the most gruesome campaigns undertaken by the Romans in Britain. Men, women and children were ruthlessly killed, while Druid priests and their followers were thrown into ditches and burned alive.

36

South Wales was a real challenge for the Romans. Powerful tribes called the Silures fought off the Roman Army for many years. The Romans managed to build a fort in Cardiff and had to send for reinforcements to conquer South Wales. Today you can visit the famous remains of the Roman camp at Caerleon, near Newport. For the Roman soldiers stationed there, it had a top-of-the-range leisure complex with heated changing rooms, warm and cold baths, a gym and a swimming pool.

At Caerleon – or Isca as it was known in Roman times – visitors today can see the amphitheatre and imagine all that blood and gore where gladiators and beasts fought tooth and claw. Down the Roman road is Venta Silurum, the first town in Wales and the tribal capital of the Silures – Caerwent today. It still has the remains of shops, a temple and the forum-basilica (a meeting place and marketplace).

Cue for a History Lesson...

Teacher: Today we're visiting a Roman forum. What is a forum?

Pupil: Er... Two-um plus two-um?

Teacher: Doh! Why did the Romans build such straight roads?

Pupil: So their soldiers didn't go round the bend.

Teacher: Look – what do you think of these fragments of Roman forum walls?

Pupil: It should look quite nice when it's all finished.

Teacher: (Big sigh) Let's do maths instead.

Scotland

The Romans were desperate to head to the far north of Britain to the land known as Caledonia (now called Scotland). The Roman Governor of Britain, called Agricola, tried to conquer Scotland in 79 AD, but the fearsome Picts wouldn't have it. By then, Rome ruled most of southern Britain – but Scotland was a much wilder place. It was still controlled by fierce warrior tribes who refused to bow to the Roman Empire.

Scotland had valuable silver and gold that the Romans wanted to mine. They also wanted to charge the people taxes and force them to be slaves. But the tribes had other ideas.

Can you make a Caesar salad?

No, but I'll have a good stab at it.

41

The Romans brought black rats to Britain, so there!

In 84 AD, Caledonian tribes joined forces and made a stand against the invading Roman army. The two sides fought in the Grampian Mountains. The Picts had 30,000 warriors, about twice as many as the Romans. Even so, the Romans were better organised and defeated the tribes. Romans 1, Picts 0.

The Picts didn't give up and kept raiding Roman forts. It was time for the Roman Emperor to get tough. I'm gonna build a wall, he said in his best Latin. (Ego aedificare murum.)

There's no need to get ratty about it.

The Emperor was Hadrian, who ruled for 21 years from 117 AD until 138 AD, when the Empire of Ancient Rome was at its height (and so was his wall). His idea was that a great wall across the north of England would keep out those pesky Picts and stop them stealing all their Roman stuff.

43

Fast Facts

1 Hadrian's Wall was 117 km (73 miles) long, 2–3 metres (6.5–10 feet) wide, and took 6 years to build.

2 Many soldiers and their families lived in settlements right beside the wall.

3 In 197 AD the wall was overrun by the barbarian Picts from the north. Many of the forts had to be rebuilt.

4 Hadrian's Wall is still intact today in many places, is a tourist attraction and can be walked along for much of its length.

Keep taking the tablets

Thin slices of oak have been found with Latin messages on them – each about the size of a postcard. These are known as the Vindolanda tablets, letters sent home from soldiers or to Roman officers serving at Vindolanda, Northumberland from 90 AD to 120 AD – just before Hadrian built his wall nearby.

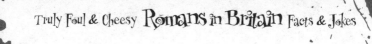

Wish You Were Here

The messages show what life was like for the Romans sent to garrisons in freezing, far-flung parts of the empire. Some officers pleaded for clothes to keep them warm through the Northumberland winter, including subuclae (vests) and abollae (thick heavy cloaks).

'Paria udonum ab Sattua solearum duo et subligariorum duo,' one soldier asks for. That's socks, two pairs of sandals and two pairs of underpants (no doubt extra thick).

The Vindolanda tablets also show what kind of food was eaten then. Officers and other rich Romans enjoyed meats such as venison and wild boar. Other soldiers ate garlic, fish, semolina, lentils, olives, olive oil and the best Italian wine. The local Picts just ate pork fat, cereal and pork scratchings washed down with beer. Healthy eating wasn't top of their list.

One message home from a miserable Roman read: 'The British sky is obscured by constant rain and cloud.' Get used to it, mate!

Did You Know?

The Romans in Britain weren't just men. Many Roman women lived in the camps along Hadrian's Wall. They were the wives, mothers, daughters and sisters of soldiers (even though ordinary soldiers weren't officially allowed to marry until 197 AD). Not many people know that.

And Now For Utter Cheesiness...

Teacher: Who can tell me where
Hadrian's Wall is?
Pupil: Around Hadrian's garden, miss.
Teacher: The Celts had to choose their
leaders carefully.
Pupil: They must have been hand-Pict.
(Better than being nose-Pict!)

A Roman soldier had enough of building roads so he ran off, hoping to escape to Scotland. As he tried to climb over Hadrian's Wall, he fell – leaving his loculus (Roman satchel) full of Roman coins stuck on the top. The big question for Roman Law was whether the soldier should be punished for desertion and stealing luggage. It took a long time to decide – after all, it's a borderline case (get it?). In fact, once the satchel had been unlocked and examined, the case was closed (an open and shut case, if ever there was one).

Q: What was Hadrian's favourite make of ice cream?
A: Walls

England

Five fast foul-free fizzing facts about Romans in Britain

1 The first Roman city in Britain was Camulodunum. Today it is the town of Colchester.

2 Many of today's cities in England were established by the Romans, including London, York, Northwich, Dover, Bath and Canterbury. Place names ending in 'cester', 'chester' or 'caster' were Roman forts or towns. How many can you name?

3 It was once thought that the Romans didn't settle much further west than Exeter in Devon, but recently Roman coins and other evidence found in Cornwall and Dartmoor suggests military camps here protected supply routes for tin.

Life in Roman Britain is becoming a rat race

Towns in Roman Britain were small by today's standards. Colchester and Cirencester probably had between 10,000 and 12,000 people, but most towns were smaller with only 3,000–5,000 people.

Roman London was the biggest city Britain would see for over a thousand years. At around 120 AD, Londinium (as it was called) was home to about 45,000 people. It would not reach that size again until the 13th century.

Bath

The city of Bath in Somerset is famous for its Roman baths, where hot spring water still bubbles naturally from the ground at 46°C (114°F). There was nothing the Romans liked better than hot water, taking a dip with friends and having a good scrub together. The Romans built bathhouses above Bath's three natural hot springs, beside a temple dedicated to the healing goddess Sulis-Minerva. The baths are now one of the best-preserved ancient Roman spas in the world.

Bathtime at the Bath baths

A million litres of hot spring water burst each day from red-stained holes in the stone walls. Wafting up from the turquoise waters would be clouds of steam and sulphur fog. The sound of plunging soldiers, some cheering, some singing, would swirl in the hot, sticky mist. Other bathers were busy talking, laughing or scrubbing, some wrestling, and at the water's edge stalls sold sausages, oysters and roasted dormice. This type of scene attracted hordes of visitors to the famous baths, including emperors, soldiers, traders, housewives and children.

After a good scrape with a curved, metal tool called a strigil, used to scrub dirt and sweat from the body, bathers could have a warm bath in the tepidarium or plunge into a cold bath called the frigidarium. The cold water closed up the skin's pores again and got the blood flowing – to give a pleasant tingling feeling afterwards. Would you be tempted to try it?

The trouble is... FOUL ALERT... although the Romans were keen on cleanliness, they didn't know too much about parasites.

Scientists have found evidence
of roundworms that lived inside
bodies, as well as parasites that lived
outside the body – lice, fleas and
bed bugs – suggesting the Romans'
bathhouses weren't keeping them
much cleaner than Britons still
living in their tribes in the forests.

Anyone fancy a
bath tonight?

57

It Gets Worse...

Archaeologists have discovered fine-toothed combs from the Roman period, probably used for removing lice from hair. Steamy bathhouses were ideal places for parasites to party. If the water wasn't changed very often, a scum from human dirt and gunge would spread over the surface – just right for microorganisms to breed. And here's another thing... (brace yourself for more GROSS), parasites lived in human poo. What did the Romans do with human poo? They spread it on fields to feed plants. This is still done today in many places, and it is good for the plants... if you first compost the poo long enough to kill off any parasite eggs. But the Romans didn't know that. Ergh!

However, to their credit, Romans did help to clean up Britain by introducing sewers, plumbing and even street cleaning. Even so – just think of those scummy baths and the lurgies lurking within. Would you still be tempted to try the waters?

London

When the Romans arrived in Britain, the commander of troops was Aulus Plautius. He marched his men from their landing place in Kent towards Colchester, their main base. The trouble was, there was a whopping great river in the way. Plautius was forced to build a bridge to get his men across the River Thames.

The Roman settlement grew on the north side of the bridge, called Londinium, which quickly became important as a trading centre for goods brought up the River Thames by boat and unloaded at wooden docks by the bridge. This first 'London Bridge' has been excavated and it's very close to the modern London Bridge.

I've just arrived by boat from Rome, to see the sights of Londinium!

Remains in the Mud

Around the year 200 AD a wall was built all around the city to keep out enemies. For well over a millennium the shape and size of London was affected by this Roman wall. The area inside the wall is now 'the City', London's famous financial area. Traces of the wall can still be seen in a few places. But that's not all. Archaeologists have dug around in London clay for years and they've unearthed all kinds of Roman remains, including human bones.

Evidence of Roman Britain's slave trade has been unearthed here: a receipt for a young French girl bought for the equivalent price of a small sports car today. Faint scratchings on a wooden writing tablet show that a wealthy household bought a girl named Fortunata (Lucky), a member of a Celtic tribe living in France. The tablet had been preserved in wet London soil for 2,000 years.

Slaves

The Romans captured many slaves in the countries they invaded. It was the same in Britain. Britons were forced to work in mines or on farms, with some given high status jobs like helping to run estates and households of wealthy Romans. In time, some slaves became rich enough to buy their own slaves – and their freedom. Others became soldiers. There were two kinds of Roman soldiers: legionaries – who were the best troops in the army – and auxiliaries, who were soldiers recruited in the lands conquered by the Romans.

Captured Celts were made to clear forests, drain swamps, build roads and quarry stone for all those Roman walls.

65

Revolting Remains

Scientists have studied skulls discovered at the London Wall, using the latest Crime Scene Science techniques at the Museum of London, where 39 skulls are kept. So why were so many severed heads of men buried in Roman London? The experts have three possible answers...

Are you wearing extra thick waterproof thermals?

It's the fall of the Roman umpire

Fallen gladiators

The most likely theory is that the men died in a local amphitheatre. Many of the skulls had injuries, suggesting death was caused by violent fights.

Executed criminals

Cutting off heads was a way of finishing off gladiators, but not everyone who died in the Roman amphitheatre was a gladiator. It was where common criminals were executed, or sometimes for entertainment two criminals would be given swords and left to kill one another. For many Romans, that made for a good day out.

Victims of Head-hunting

Another idea is that the skulls are the heads of Scottish barbarians killed by Roman forces and brought to London as trophies. There is evidence of head-taking from across the Roman empire, and heads are shown being held up in triumph on the tombstones of cavalry officers in Britain. It would have taken weeks to take them all the way from Scotland to London, and not very nice if a sack of smelly heads ripped open on the way. That's enough to make a Roman lose his head!

York

The major Roman city in the north of England grew up after 5,000 soldiers of the Ninth Legion marched from Lincoln and set up camp in around 71 AD. York was then called Eboracum, and it became an important northern centre.

Historians have picked over Roman remains in York and have discovered many foul facts. They uncovered an entire cemetery of gladiators.

Gladiators – a quick reminder

Gladiators were armed fighters (from the Latin word 'gladius' for sword), who fought against each other, condemned criminals and wild animals. In most cases, they fought till one of them accepted defeat or was killed. Gladiators fought for the entertainment of the public. People filled a stadium or amphitheatre to cheer on the gladiators fighting to the death in the arena. Those with ringside seats would risk getting splashed with blood, but that was all part of the fun, so they thought.

I can't bear the sight of blood...

Gruesome discovery

The 2,000-year-old remains of almost 80 young men were found by archaeologists as they excavated an area of York. At first, it seemed the men were the victims of a mass execution. Then scientists got to work (look away now)...

Shall we have an Italian tonight?

The men's injuries included severed heads and even a tiger bite on at least one skeleton – suggesting they were gladiators who met a gruesome end entertaining the bloodthirsty crowds. Some skeletons showed healed injuries from weapons, and all men were described as tall and fit (apart from being dead). Their skeletons showed signs they were heavily muscled from weapons training. The men had suffered many injuries, including hammer blows to the head – a method for a gladiator to finish off an opponent.

We can be sure the Romans brought gladiator fighting to Britain and built arenas and amphitheatres in important Roman cities including London, York and Chester.

Chester

Other gruesome remains have been unearthed at the arena in Chester. In Roman times Chester was known as Castra Deva, meaning 'the military camp on the River Dee'.

This town also saw grisly fights to the death for public entertainment.

Have you ever had one of those days?

A stone block with iron fittings was discovered at the centre of the two-storey amphitheatre, which dates to about 100 AD. Like other stone blocks found at the site, it was probably put around the arena to prevent gladiators from sheltering against the arena wall and not giving spectators such a good view of the action. Chaining victims to these blocks was thought to be more fun for the audience – but grim for the gladiators.

ARRGHHH!

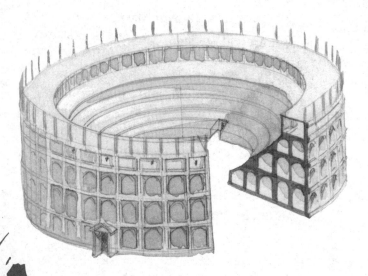

Archaeologists cannot be sure exactly what types of gladiator entertainment went on in Chester, but it was most likely that a type of gladiator called a bestiaries (trained to fight savage animals) did battle here. The Chester amphitheatre was rebuilt about 100 years after it was first used – to resemble a scaled-down version of Rome's Colosseum.

Did you know?

There were female gladiators (gladiatrix or gladiatrices) in Ancient Rome. Although they were very rare, written records and archaeological evidence shows they did exist. They probably entertained the crowds in Britain, too. Archaeologists from the Museum of London believe they discovered the first known burial site of a female Roman gladiator in Southwark, south London. She had been cremated and given a special funeral. Maybe she was a big star of her time.

I'm a celebrity - get me out of here!

Have you done a risk assessment?

And another thing...

The life of a gladiator in Britain wasn't much better than a highly-prized slave. Not many gladiators would survive more than ten matches, and few would ever live longer than 30 years old. It's thought that up to one million gladiators may have been killed in contests across the Roman Empire. Such 'sport' was popular in Roman Britain, when contests would often begin with the execution of prisoners, who were thrown to the lions, tigers or bears. The cheering crowd would go wild as the gladiators were paraded around before the fight.

Gladiators were chosen from young criminals, enemy soldiers or slaves, and trained in different styles of fighting – like aiming their swords at the major arteries of an opponent and... (you can imagine the next bit!)

79

- FOUL ALERT -

If a gladiator was killed, the crowd would go crazy. There would often be a rush of sick people who would try to drink his blood and nibble his liver. They believed this would make them strong and fit. But that's not all. Women who were desperate for eternal youth collected the sweat and dead skin scrapings from gladiators, and worked them into a facial cream. It was rubbed all over the woman's face in the hope it would make her look gorgeous and **DEAD ROMAN**tic (get it?).

EXTRA

Foul alert...

When Romans weren't swigging gladiator blood, some gulped down a sweet energy drink containing goat dung. Charioteers were known to boil goat dung and vinegar into a drink or grind it into a powder. They gulped it down as a pick-me-up when they were exhausted. In fact, one of the most well-known lovers of goat dung refreshment was the crazy Emperor Nero. He must have had revoltingly bad breath.

Roman 1: I don't like to gossip – but I heard the emperor killed his mother.

Roman 2: I'm not surprised. She was a terrible woman and very wicked.

Roman 1: He had her cooked and served up for supper.

Roman 2: In that case, I'm gladiator! (glad-he-ate-her)

Roman 1: Doh!

Despite that terrible joke, we'd better soldier on.

Bad Joke

Did you hear about the gladiator who was having a rough day at the arena? His opponent had sliced off both of his arms. Nevertheless, he fought on, kicking and biting as furiously as he could. But when his opponent lopped off both feet, the gladiator had no choice but to give up. He was now both un-armed and de-feet-ed.

Revolting Limericks

Romans were a
bloodthirsty bunch
Who'd cheer at a kick
or a punch,
When they went as
spectators
To admire gladiators
Who chopped their
opponents with a crunch.

The Romans could be very
vicious,
Swordfighters were tough
and ambitious.
It was 'kill or be killed'
So if they weren't skilled
They'd be served up on toast
– how delicious!
(Maybe not literally – but
you get the gist)

NEXT!

I'M A GLADIATOR...
GET ME OUT OF HERE!

An Ancient Roman Game
Show with presenters Antius
and Decorus

Decorus: Welcome to I'm A Gladiator Get Me Out of Here, where we're down to our last contestants. Today's vote will decide this year's BFG winner – The Britannia Fortunium Gadiatorus – that's the British Tournament of Gladiators. It could be quite a messy fight, isn't that so, Antius?

Antius: That's right, Decorus. As always, the losers will be fed to the lions.

Decorus: Great! But before that, let's find out what grisly challenges await our gladiators this week in the Londinium Amphitheatre Arena. And you know what that means?

Antius: Of course I know what that means. Arena means 'sand' because that's what's on the floor (it helps to soak up the blood). It means we're in for some great fun – so long as you're not a gladiator.

Decorus: We'd better get started.

Antius: It's time to see what's in the arena for tonight's show. Could it be a gladiator and a barber? Do you know the difference between a mad gladiator and his barber?

Antius: I don't know. What is the difference between a mad gladiator and his barber?

Decorus: One's a raving showman, the other's a shaving Roman!

Antius: I wish I hadn't asked. Look, the gladiators are entering the arena and raising their arms...

Gladiators: Ave, Caesar! Morituri te salutamus!

Antius: That means 'Hail, Caesar! We who are about to die salute you!'

Decorus: Shouldn't they also shout 'Stand and de-liver'?

Antius: Ah yes, as some spectators like to cut out a dead gladiator's liver. Eating it is meant to make you strong and brave. Some people believe that drinking the warm blood of a dead gladiator makes you feel great.

Decorus: Yuk. I'm glad I've got a flask of tea and a bag of chips.

Antius: But listen up, gladiators. Here are your tasks... Your challenge will be completely armless.

Decorus: It won't be very exciting if it's harmless.

Antius: No, not harmless. Armless. They'll be unarmed. No weapons allowed.

Decorus: No weapons. No shields. No armour.

Who wants a bear knuckle fight?

Antius: You will all stand in the middle of the arena totally defenceless while wild and hungry beasts are released. The audience will be gambling on which of you will last the longest.

Decorus: The first animals you have to fight are wild bears. Big ones. You'll have a bear charging at you from the front and a bear behind.

Antius: A bear behind? By the way, not many people know this, but Caesar has a giraffe which is said to be part camel, part leopard – a camelopardalis. That's true, you know.

Decorus: Once they've dealt with the bears, there will be tigers. Big hungry ones.

Antius: The Emperor is the referee. He's about to sit down – yikes, he's just slipped off his chair.

Decorus: It's the fall of the Roman Umpire!

Antius: The gladiators may fight the bears with tridents and swords next.

Decorus: I can't BEAR the suspense, but now we've got to take a break.

91

Antius: We'll be back to find out what happens next.

Decorus: How will you cast your votes to decide who is this week's winner of I'm A Gladiator Get Me Out Of Here? Which one of our contestants do you think should win The Gadiatorus Maximus Prize? Er… Antius…

Antius: Yes, Decorus?

WAAAHHooo!

Roar!

Decorus: Don't look now but a bear has escaped and it's just behind us...

Antius: Yikes! On that breaking news, we must leave you with the shocking image of another bear behind.

(They both run off screaming.)

The Romans Leave

and Rome falls

For over 350 years, Britain had been an important part of the Roman Empire. After 250 AD, the Romans were having more problems in managing all their territories. Attacks from enemies outside the empire put Rome under increasing strain. By 410 AD, the Romans could no longer rule Britain because they were needed back home to defend Italy. They had to leave Britons to defend themselves against foreign enemies. So, the Romans departed at last. With no army to defend them, the British people were soon attacked by other invaders when the Anglo Saxons arrived. That's another story.

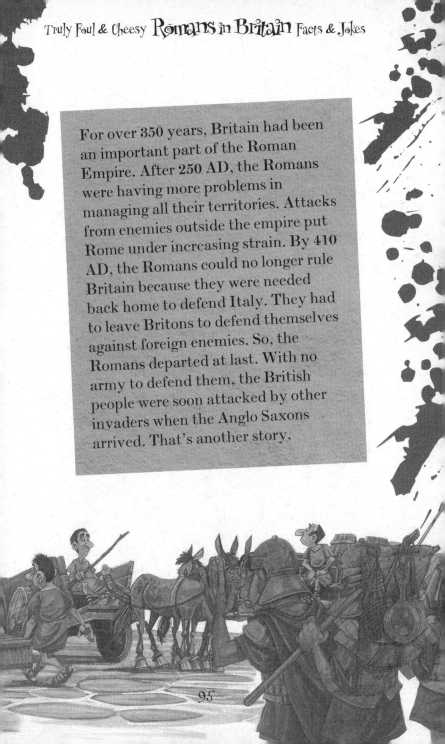

The Romans left a lot behind in Britain – not just what they'd built but so many other things that are still part of British life.

Foul or Fab?

Depending on your personal taste, you'll either thank or blame the Romans for bringing these foods to Britain: garlic, onions, shallots, leeks, peas, celery, turnips, radishes, walnuts, asparagus and (take a deep breath) probably brussel sprouts. How many get your vote?

The Romans also introduced apples, grapes, mulberries and cherries, as well as chickens, pheasants, hares and rabbits.

Apart from amazingly straight roads, the Romans also left us with:

1 central heating

2 concrete

3 aqueducts (bridges for water)

4 censuses (to count how many people there are in a country every few years)

Language

Many of the words we use today in English are based on Latin words used by the Romans. We use words like 'exit', which means 'he or she goes out', and 'pedestrian', which means 'going on foot'. Romans knew all about that.

When the Romans first arrived in Britain, very few people could read or write a single word. Instead, information was passed from person to person by word of mouth. But the Romans wrote down their history, their literature and their laws. Their Latin language caught on in the new Roman towns – although most people living in the countryside stuck to their old Celtic language.

Did You Know?

Our coins are based on a Roman design and some of the lettering is in Latin. Written around the edge of some £1 coins is the phrase 'decus et tutamen' which means 'glory and protection'.

Rat bones were found in London's Roman remains. True - no bones about it.

How About a Date?

The calendar we use today was started by Julius Caesar and is based on the movement of the earth around the sun, and so is called the 'solar calendar.' The solar calendar has 365 days a year, and 366 days every leap year, or every fourth year. The names of our months are taken from the names of Roman gods and rulers. The month 'July' is named after Julius Caesar, while August is named after his great nephew, the Emperor Augustus Caesar. So if your birthday is in July or August, you've got those Roman rulers to thank!

Roman Numbers

Keep a lookout for Roman numerals, as we still use them all over the place, even though some people get a bit muddled by them. So just to help you out, here's all you need...

It all looks Greek to me!.

Roman numerals

I	II	III	IV	V
1	2	3	4	5
VI	VII	VIII	IX	X
6	7	8	9	10
XI	XII	XIII	XIV	XV
11	12	13	14	15
XVI	XVII	XVIII	XIX	XX
16	17	18	19	20
XXX	XL	L	LX	LXX
30	40	50	60	70
LXXX	XC	C	CXXV	CC
80	90	100	125	200
D	M	MM	$\overline{V}$	$\overline{X}$
500	1000	2000	5000	10000

Number Fun Time

I, for one, understand Roman numerals. Do you II?

A Roman walks into a bakery, holds up two fingers and says, 'I'll have five rolls please and a hot X bun.' He got 10 of those!

I can't remember what 51, 6 and 500 are in Roman numerals. That makes me LIVID.

1st Roman Soldier: What's the time?
2nd Roman Soldier: XX past VII.
1st Roman Soldier: That means it's time for
                    The X Factor.
2nd Roman Soldier: Yeah – it's the best
                    Roman sun cream you
                    can get.

I VIII your pasta.

I'll never IV-give you.

The Romans Return

Just when you thought the ancient Romans left Britain for good over 1,600 years ago... they're back! WARNING - it's best not to read the next bit after dark. It could turn scary.

From time to time people report seeing ghosts of Roman troops on the march along our ancient Roman roads. Or how about this story from 1953 in York...

One morning in 1953, a trainee plumber called Harry Martindale was fitting new central heating pipes in the cellars of the Treasurer's House when he heard a sound like a distant trumpet. He thought it was a bit strange but carried on working up his ladder. The trumpet sounded louder and seemed to be coming closer.

Suddenly a huge cart horse emerged straight through the brick wall of the cellar! Harry fell off his ladder in shock and, as he crouched on the floor, he could clearly see the horse was being ridden by a Roman soldier. More soldiers followed, all dressed in green tunics and plumed helmets, carrying short swords and spears. At first it seemed as if they were on their knees but then they reached an excavated area, where they were walking on the old Roman road buried below the surface.

Harry scrambled frantically up the cellar steps to the ground floor. Here he was met by the house's curator who said, 'You've seen the Roman soldiers, haven't you?'

Apparently, the ghostly troop had been seen several times before by many stunned witnesses. Yikes! The cellar is sometimes open to the public ... if you dare. But don't have too many nightmares.

Timeline
(Year AD)

43 The Roman Emperor Claudius orders four legions to conquer Britain (A full strength legion was officially made up of 6,000 soldiers called legionnaires.)

48 The Romans have now conquered all territory between the Humber Estuary and the Severn Estuary. Parts that remain under British control are Wales, Scotland and the North West of England.

60 The Romans attack the Druid stronghold of Anglesey.

61 Boudicca leads a rebellion of the Iceni tribe of East Anglia against the Romans. After burning down Colchester, London and St Albans, Boudicca is eventually defeated at the Battle of Watling Street.

108

80 London has grown into a large town with a forum, basilica, governor's palace and even an amphitheatre.

 84 The Romans head further north to battle with the Caledonians in Scotland.

 **100** Most of the 8,000 miles of Roman roads in Britain are completed, allowing troops and goods to travel easily across the country.

Did you know Romans call us rattus rattus?

Maybe because there are two of us.

 To strengthen the border between Roman-occupied Britain and Scotland, Emperor Hadrian orders the building of a wall.

 The Antonine Wall in Scotland is built, moving the northern border of Roman-occupied Britain.

 Villas start appearing across the British countryside, some with mosaic floors.

 After years of conflict with the northern tribes, the Romans lead an army to Hadrian's Wall border to sort out the Caledonians. Eventually peace treaties are signed.

211 Britain is divided into two separate provinces; the south to be called 'Britannia Superior' (as it's closer to Rome), with the north being named 'Britannia Inferior'. London is the new capital of the south, with York the capital of the north.

I'll pay you with salt. (Yes, Romans did this.)

 **250 onwards** New threats to Roman Britannia emerge as the Picts from Scotland, as well as the Angles, Saxons and Jutes from Germany and Scandinavia, start threatening Roman lands.

 **255** With the increasing threat from overseas tribes, London's city wall is completed with the final stretch along the north bank of the Thames.

 **287** The admiral of the Roman Channel fleet, Carausius, declares himself Emperor of Britain and starts minting his own coins.

 314 Christianity becomes legal in the Roman Empire.

 **367** Barbarians from Scotland, Ireland and Germany launch raids on Roman Britain. Many towns are plundered and Britain falls into disorder.

 Large-scale Barbarian attacks on Britain start up again.

 Peace is fully restored throughout Roman Britannia.

 With the Roman Empire focused on serious threats to Italy, reinforcements have stopped and Britain is left to its own devices.

 With increased attacks from the Saxons, Scots, Picts and Angles, Britain turns to the Roman Emperor Honorius for help. He writes back telling them to 'look to their own defences', and refuses to send any help. This letter marked the end of Roman Britain. The Romans return to Rome and the great empire crumbles within 66 years.

And Finally...

No, not pants but a subligaculum! This was a kind of underwear worn by ancient Romans. It could be a bit like a pair of shorts, or a simple loincloth, and was worn by men and women. It was part of the dress of gladiators, athletes and of actors on the stage (but a bit draughty in those chilly British winters). So just remember... never get your subligaculum in a twist.

A word of warning to any armies out there wanting to invade Britain today. Just remember the words from Julius Caesar about the scary people of Britain who look blue, with weird tattoos 'and thereby have a more terrible appearance in fight. They wear their hair long, and have every part of their body shaved except their head and upper lip.' Just watch out – many still do. Ever seen Chelsea play at home?

[If you survived some of the truly foul facts and cheesy jokes in this book, take a look at the other wacky titles in this revolting series. They're all guaranteed to make you groan and squirm like never before. Share them with your friends AT YOUR OWN RISK!]

QUIZ

Page 116 and approaching a quiz, mate!

1. WHat does the Greek word 'keltoi' mean?

a) Hairy

b) Barbarian

c) Dangerous

Have you seen the dormouse pasta?

2. In what year was the Roman emperor Romulus Augustus defeated by the German Goth Odoacer?

a) 476 AD

b) 385 AD

c) 1997 AD

3. What is the name of the bluish dye native Britons painted themselves with?

a) Woad

b) Alizarin

c) Cresyl

4. What language did Romans speak and write?

a) Welsh

b) Italian

c) Latin

5. What did Romans use to wipe their bottoms?

a) Andrex

b) Stray cats

c) A sponge on a stick

6. What did 'Britannia' mean in Latin?

a) Land of spray tans

b) Land of tin

c) Land of terrible weather

7. Who led the Celtic tribes against the Roman invaders in 60 AD?

a) Queen Boudicca

b) King Canute

c) Alfred the Great

8. What did the audience sometimes do when a gladiator was killed?

a) Try to give CPR

b) Drink his blood

c) Get a selfie with the corpse

These questions are far too cheesy!

Fighting you is child's play!

9. Which Roman emperor built a wall across the north of England to keep out the Picts?

a) Hadrian

b) Augustus

c) Julian

10. What was the name for a warm Roman bath?

a) Jacuzzi

b) Frigidarium

c) Tepidarium

GLOSSARY

Ammonia: a mixture of nitrogen and hydrogen, often used as a cleaning fluid.

Archaeologist: a person who studies excavated sites and artefacts to find out about past civilisations.

Britons: the native people of Britain who lived on the island before the arrival of the Romans and, later, the Anglo-Saxons.

Cereal: grains that are used for human food, such as wheat or maize.

Goths: A Germanic people from Scandinavia who frequently attacked and engaged in warfare with the Roman Empire.

Julius Caesar: Roman general and dictator who ruled the Roman Empire until his assassination in 44 BC.

Mosaic: a picture or pattern made by sticking together lots of small pieces of tile, stone or glass.

Villa: a large country house, formed of farm and domestic buildings around a central courtyard.

INDEX

I finished reading this Truly
Foul & Cheesy book on:

........../.........../..........